WHY
SELL
TACOS
IN AFRICA?

WHY
SELL
TACOS
IN AFRICA?

PAUL ØBERSCHNEIDER

WHY SELL TACOS IN AFRICA

Cover design by Popcorn Design
www.popcorndesign.co.uk

Interior layout and typesetting by Atthis Arts LLC
www.atthisarts.com

Editorial services by Quill Pen Editorial
www.quillpeneditorial.com

Published by Harriman House Ltd
www.harriman-house.com

Visit pauloberschneider.com for more information.

ISBN 978-0-9957630-0-5

" Most people think the pennies take care of the dollars.
Entrepreneurs think the dollars take care of the pennies.
If you do everything like everyone else you will get the same
results. "

PAUL ⊘BERSCHNEIDER

TABLE OF CONTENTS

INTRODUCTION

T HE TITLE OF THIS BOOK might make you think it's about doing business in Africa. It's not.

Then again, maybe it is. But that's not how it started.

The title of the book is a metaphor for finding opportunities to build businesses in blue-sky markets—markets where there is very little competition and the tide can carry you to riches. It's hard to find tacos in Africa, which means an entrepreneur who starts a Mexican restaurant in Ghana or Nigeria won't face the same stiff competition they'd encounter in L.A. The title helps me explain how I made my fortune in the post-Soviet countries of Central and Eastern Europe from 1992 to 2008. I started from nothing and built a great portfolio of companies in an emerging market.

My intent is to help people who want to start or grow a business by passing on the lessons I've learned over the course of eighteen years.

Leaving behind my past as a Chicago and Wall Street floor trader, I arrived in Estonia in 1992 with $400 in my worn blue jeans pocket. I had set off on a journey to start my life over. I hadn't planned to start a business.

But by the end of that summer, a surprising turn of events led to my stuffing $100,000 in earned banknotes in shoeboxes under the bed of my rented Soviet-era apartment. That was the start of everything.

Instead of heading back home like everyone—including myself—had expected, I stayed to help a friend start a bank. And over the course of eighteen years, I created one of the largest real estate companies in Central and Eastern Europe—building shopping centers, residential homes, and five-star boutique hotels frequented by politicians and celebrities across Eastern Europe. I was riding the back of a killer wave of liquidity rushing over the small, wild markets of the former Soviet Union.

One evening at a sauna party in 1992, I met a businessman who called himself "Elvis." He warned me to never commit to a deal if Finnish businessmen showed interest because they always entered the market too late. Naturally, I forgot that comment for eighteen years.

Years later, that casual conversation came back to me when a Finnish private equity firm wanted to buy one of my businesses. My property development firm was booming. I was running around London lining up investors for a Central and Eastern European property fund, and I wanted to purchase a publicly traded company in Helsinki. That sauna conversation came flashing back, and alarm bells rang in my head.

With just a hunch, despite an explosive market, I made the sudden decision to fold and sell all my businesses one by one. Just as the last business sold in 2008, the crisis hit, and the economy crashed. The music stopped, and I was out when the values plummeted. I was suddenly a guru.

Back in 1987, when I was a New York trader who partied all night and rolled up to his desk still inebriated to trade hundreds of thousands of dollars, I woke up to find myself destitute, broke, and lost. At that moment, I couldn't have been further away from a prosperous entrepreneurial future. Yet that is where my journey took me.

I want to share some of the things I discovered on that journey. Forget the "Ten Secrets to Success." The real secret is that I took a different path and found blue sky—a market where I could thrive and where there was very little competition. Like selling tacos in Africa.

I went into countries I knew nothing about, where I didn't even speak the language. I started with $400 and built businesses worth $200 million.

I've written this book to share how I did that so others can learn. Building a successful business takes time. It's a process, not an overnight transformation. I know of no overnight successes. During the process, I built a great team that was like my family. We created things. We achieved tangible results we could point to. Those results made us all a lot of money—and we had fun doing it.

What I did never felt like work. It was better than a hobby. We went in early and left late because we didn't want to stop having fun. That's what we are all trying to achieve in life, I think—an exciting journey with great friends where we're having fun and making a difference.

Remember the story of Jack and the Beanstalk? Poor and destitute, Jack's mom asks him to go sell the cow for money to buy food. Jack, young and impressionable, gets conned and ends up taking the money and buying some "magic beans." When he comes home, he is sent to his room. He falls asleep and dreams of great riches in the sky at the end of the giant beanstalk. Of course, we all know that when he woke up, they still had no food, and the beans his mother threw out the window would produce only more beans.

We all want to believe Jack's dream. We all want things to happen right now.

But the journey is a process. It's like a puzzle, and you won't know exactly where all the pieces fit quite yet. Entrepreneurship is about exploration, about finding where the pieces fit. There are puzzle pieces called strategies, and there is an underlying mindset that you will need in order to successfully start and grow any business. I want to share with you what worked for me.

It's easy to be lured by get-rich formulas promising things that can't be delivered. And maybe you've already had your fingers burned with the painful trial-and-error methods of those schemes.

My book makes no promises; I have no "magic beans" to sell you. In these pages, I'll tell my story and share what worked for me. I believe it can probably work for you, too. It is a collection of paths I took that may help you build a successful business, and I truly hope you achieve your dreams as you apply the lessons. Remember, it's an exploration.

But while I was writing the next sixteen chapters, something else happened. The book title and its original purpose took on a different meaning for me after I met a complete stranger in a Chelsea café on Sloan Square in London. That meeting has challenged me to an even greater undertaking. As I've distilled the elements that led to my success into sixteen simple, easy-to-grasp concepts, I've been inspired to set out on a new adventure of my own.

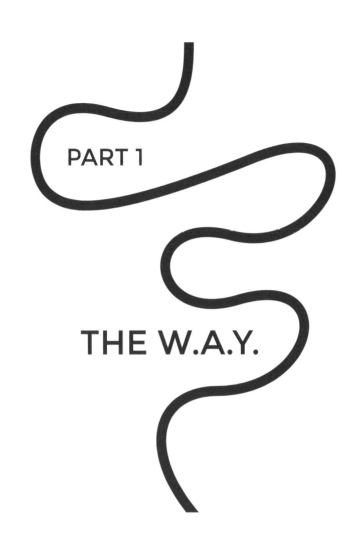

PART 1

THE W.A.Y.

THE START OF MY ADVENTURE

IN 1992, MY FRIEND ROGER dropped me off at Kennedy Airport in New York. It was an unusually hot New York day, and the air conditioning wasn't working in his brand new 4x4. I'd quit smoking two weeks earlier, so I was a bit edgy. The two deli coffees swirling in my gut sure didn't help. Roger and I had been friends for a long time. We'd met in 1987 and had been through a lot together. We said our goodbyes and gave each other an awkward hug at the departure drop-off. I had one bag and $400 in my pocket, and I was now off on what would be a life-changing journey.

From 1982 to 1987, I'd traveled a wild and rocky road on Wall Street. My five years as a young futures trader had been stressful and physically demanding—and to deal with that stress, I played hard. I was young and impressionable, and like a kid unsupervised in a candy store, I was taken in by all the temptations a big city could offer. I gobbled up as much as I could. The whole thing nearly killed me. By 1987, I was done. I felt burned out and unfulfilled. To top it all off, I was broke.

When Roger dropped me off at the airport, I was thirty-three years old, and I'd spent six years recovering from my addictions and alcoholism. I felt I was ready to start my life and career all over again, but I was as far from being a successful business leader and multi-millionaire entrepreneur as anyone could be. I was really at the bottom.

I'd been fired from Wall Street. At best, I was a lost soul. But deep down, when I looked at myself in the mirror each day, I knew I wanted to do something meaningful with my life. I just didn't know what. All I saw was uncertainty and a lot of unpaid bills, which I conveniently stashed out of view in a box on my desk.

Everything changed when I decided to visit the small Eastern European country of Estonia, where my dad had emigrated from after the Second World War. I put all my stuff in storage and sold my possessions (which were few). With my last remaining $400 in my wallet (acquired through the sale of a computer to my girlfriend) and a practically unused passport, I boarded a Finnair flight and left America.

Most people think they need to get from A to Z in a straight line—as the crow flies. And, of course, a lot of people out there say they can do that for you. I wish it were that easy. But then again, if it were that easy, life would be pretty boring. If I do *this*, I get *this*, and then *that* happens—job done! How boring is that?

Never underestimate what life might have in store for you. In 1992, I was still a fragile kid, new to sobriety, without any money or any real skills that I could think of. At least that's what I saw. But God had other plans for me, as I would find out.

I believe that successful people—in this case, people who build successful businesses—are driven by circumstances and then led by opportunity. I like the acronym W.A.Y. for "Where Are You?" Without knowing it, my trip to Estonia in 1992 was the circumstance that drove the opportunities that would find me. By 2008, I had built seven companies, helped start a bank and a mortgage company, and developed the largest retail and commercial real estate company in the region. And I was one of the largest property developers in Eastern Europe, building over two million square feet of retail space. I mean, how did that happen, really? My goal had been to go back to school and get a business degree—that was my A-to-Z plan, my magic beans.

But I missed that goal by a mile. Thinking about it now, I skipped business school because it wasn't ever really my goal. It seemed like a box I should tick off, but it wasn't my passion. That's what exploring and asking yourself "Where are you?" does—it makes some things clear without you even knowing it. After I decided to bypass business school, I ultimately ended up in a far better place, achieving the true goal I'd wanted all along.

Over a period of eighteen years, I became truly *me*—a leader of a great company with a great group of people. My small band of pirates helped me night and day, and together we built a remarkable set of businesses. At my peak, I had 850 employees in a network that spanned six countries. We all helped each other, and we all shared in the spoils. We were like family, with me at the head table.

But no matter what the circumstances, there are some essential skills every entrepreneur innately possesses. We all have them. It's just a matter of how circumstances bring them out of us and how willing we are to let go and just let shit happen.

Sure, if you want to be successful, you need to have some idea of where you want to go. But you should always be open to the reality that you might end up somewhere else. What matters is that you have an idea of where you are and where you are going. You'll probably end up somewhere better than your original plan.

Don't get me wrong—there are those days when I admire the guys who commute to work each day, have a job title, take vacations at the same time every year, and get a steady paycheck. It's predictable. But it's an illusion. Many of those people feel trapped like I did. Maybe they have a good salary and a steady job, but they are unhappy. These people will never take that leap of faith, no matter how big the pot of gold.

I still have plenty of days when everything seems to go wrong, and I just want to scream and quit—but that's the price you pay when you are in business for yourself. So if you're not successful yet and want to be, stop watching the same movie over and over again. Get out of your comfort zone and go in another direction. You must firmly believe that success is right around the corner whether you can see it or not. A successful entrepreneur I know always says, "Don't leave before the miracle happens." I have always believed in miracles. As an entrepreneur, you must be first and foremost an optimist.

For those who are game, who are willing to take risks and go against the grain, you can find freedom and earn a sense of accomplishment. And it can make you rich. I will show you that anyone who wants to pay that price can get there if they follow a few simple steps. If I can do it, anyone can. For twenty-nine years, I made every mistake you could make. But I've also found that success leaves footprints.

If you are an entrepreneur or business owner growing your company, you are a unique breed of person. If you are looking to make changes to your life, you are ready. But like anything, you need to put in the time. And like me, you'll have to do things you don't like to do. I've had to fund businesses that weren't working, step on suppliers, and stretch cash flow. I've kicked the supplier can down the road many times. I've had guns pulled on me and investors let me down. And all of this while fighting to keep my vision and trying to inspire my team. But I wouldn't have wanted it any other way. All these things have made me who I am. I'm confident that you could drop me anywhere in the world today with $400, and I could start again.

OK, probably you're not going to pack up your family and move continents like I did. Fair enough. You don't have to leave your country or your neighborhood or change your existing business right away. But you need to look at W.A.Y., understand what you're doing and expecting, and generally know where you want to go. Then you need to get up, get moving, and share that dream with others.

I SAW IT FIRST

IN THE EIGHTEEN YEARS from when I left New York for Eastern Europe, I lived out what I'd envisioned so many years before. I just didn't know that was what was happening as I was living it. Without my consciously knowing it, each step I took was part of a script I was writing for myself.

Today, as I look at the press clippings, photos, and magazine covers of all that I've achieved, I wonder, "Did that really happen? Was that really me?" But it did happen. But was it luck? Did I really do all those amazing things and make all that money? It now seems so long ago. Sitting in my office looking at press clippings or waxing on at a cocktail party to someone fascinated with my story, I wonder. I ask myself that question a lot these days. Of course, I'd like to think it was me.

As a kid growing up in Illinois in the 1960s, I saw shopping centers popping up in cornfields. I was fascinated by those big structures and all the machinery that erected them. I remember sitting astride my bike on a hilltop overlooking Turner's cornfield down the road from our house. Below me, Chicagoland's first indoor shopping mall rose up from that farmland. Somewhere in the back of my seven-year-old mind, I decided that's what I wanted to do. I wanted to build. But then I forgot.

All my life, I wanted to be able to point at the things I did. At the close of trading on Wall Street, all that remained were my trading sheets and crumpled-up order sheets—just numbers. The money earned and lost meant nothing. I wanted to do better with my life, I thought. Deep down, I wanted to own my own business, be the boss, and build stuff. I wanted to be an entrepreneur. To do things better—my way.

Being a successful entrepreneur requires three things: vision, leadership, and a team. Let me try to summarize it briefly:

1.   To be an entrepreneur, you need to be a leader.
2.   To be a leader, you need a team.
3.   To build a team, you must share your vision.
4.   All entrepreneurs have a vision.

It's not a straight line from A to Z. But you do need to know your end goal. Start with that vision, and share it as best as you can every day. If you do that, you will find the right employees, and your employees will sacrifice everything when you ask them to. Your employees are your assets. Nurture them, guide them, and help them believe in you.

You don't need to know how to do everything. Your job is to know your plan and communicate it with clarity and enthusiasm. If you wait for the 10,000-Hour Rule (meaning you need 10,000 hours of experience to be an expert), you will wait a long time. But you can hire 10,000 hours' worth of experience in a day. Most people just don't think that way.

I built over two million square feet of retail shopping center space, five hotels, countless restaurants and fast food chains, and the largest real estate company in Central and Eastern Europe. But ask me about building shopping centers, and I would probably give you pretty disappointing advice. Or ask me about kitchen fit-out or procurement for hotels—I know nothing about these things. I know very little, and that's just fine. Practically speaking, my managers and project managers built those shopping centers and hotels. I had the idea and found the people to make it all happen—that's the role of a leader.

HERE'S THE DEAL

When I arrived in Estonia, I met a young Russian on the square. His name was Sergei.

After a few days, Sergei asked me to help him write a business plan for a new shop he wanted to open. He needed a loan from the bank and didn't know how to write one. So I wrote it for him. He got the loan, asked me how much I wanted, and paid me $500.

The next week, his friend came and asked me the same question. I wrote another business plan, and he got the loan. This time, when he asked me what he owed me, I asked for $1,000. I'm not stupid. He paid me. That's how it all started.

From that single idea, I came up with a vision for a pan-Central-Eastern-European real estate group and started writing what would become my personal business plan. I still have that plan, and it looks a bit silly with all the photos I cut and pasted in, but it was the start of a written plan that I updated every year for many years. Writing it all down, having that vision, and articulating it for my team was critical. It is what everyone rallied around. And it worked. That single business grew into the largest real estate company in Central and Eastern Europe. It happened one step at a time, starting with writing Sergei's business plans until I was creating my own.

In the beginning, I had no vision. I was taking steps along a path, like wandering around a map. But once I had the vision of what I really wanted to do, everything became easy. I was able to write it up, and once I got the story down in my own mind, it was easy for me to share that story. Because I was excited, other people got excited too.

ACTIONS TO TAKE

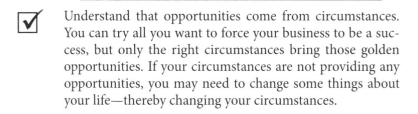

Understand that opportunities come from circumstances. You can try all you want to force your business to be a success, but only the right circumstances bring those golden opportunities. If your circumstances are not providing any opportunities, you may need to change some things about your life—thereby changing your circumstances.

Look carefully at the W.A.Y. ("Where Are You?") now. What unique circumstances are you part of? Capitalize on the opportunities your circumstances provide, and don't strive for goals that ignore your circumstances.

Wait and be patient. Don't force things. Just show up and be open-minded. As you watch the people and businesses around you, you'll start to see the available opportunities and figure out what excites your imagination.

When you find your vision, let it sink in, and see if it still excites you in a week or so. If it does, write it down into an exciting story.

Share your excitement with others, and tell your story. As you hone both your vision and your storytelling skills, you'll inspire a team to gather around you and your vision. This team is vital to your success.

My Notes

_____

_____

_____

_____

_____

_____

_____

_____

_____

_____

_____

_____

_____

_____

_____

_____

_____

_____

LEADERS ARE BELIEVERS

WE ALL BELIEVE in something when things get tough. Back in high school, my understanding of God came from praying at the toilet bowl, promising I'd never drink again if he would stop my head from spinning. Some of us know what I'm talking about. Of course, for a long time, my prayers were never answered, and I never kept my promises to God either.

Joking aside, today I feel quite strongly that a spiritual foundation and a belief in a power greater than yourself is paramount if you are to be a successful entrepreneur. At least it was for me. Before I came to that belief, I struggled. I thought I had to control everything and everyone. I pushed and pushed, trying to force things to work. And I wasn't doing a good job of it. I was constantly up against the wall; I blamed everyone and everything. I was always exhausted. Finally, I realized I needed to find another way, and that way was a leap of faith and trust. I no longer push; I pull opportunities and people to me.

Some days that's harder than others. Like when a couple of Russians came into my office and pointed a gun at me to try to force me to give them my real estate or when the city council tried to reverse my auction win of the Tallinn Harbor and sue me. And there were times I was simply overwhelmed by bureaucracy and the struggle of working in several culturally and linguistically different countries. In those times, the only thing that got me out of bed each morning was trust that I was doing the right thing and that somehow I would be taken care of.

HERE'S THE DEAL

The first thing is to believe in something—call it God, a group of colleagues, your family, school, or even your business idea. Leaders are believers:

1. You have to believe in something outside yourself. You can't control everything, so you need to trust in something. When I lost everything, I had to resign myself to the fact that I couldn't control anything or anybody except myself. You can only control how you respond to things. That's it. Trust me on this one.
2. Second, you also need to believe in yourself and whatever you choose to do. Whatever that is, it is the thing you are meant to do. If you determine you were meant to do something, any obstacle is just an inconvenient annoyance you can overcome.

Are you confident enough to believe, take center stage, and ask life for everything? Or are you sitting in the back mezzanine section just watching the show? For me to get started, I needed to find that faith and take to the stage with all the lights bearing down on me. That can be a scary idea.

In business, as in life, things change, sands shift, and suddenly everything can go wrong. But if you believe that your goal is right around the corner, you can stampede through the bandits of your mind. Faith blinds you to "it can't be done." It gives you that craziness that keeps you going. Faith protects you from naysayers and well-meaning friends who don't want you to change.

In 1992, when I landed in Tallinn on my adventure, I had no idea what my plans were going to be; I didn't know how things would work out. The only thing I knew for certain was that they *would* work out.

I landed in a dingy, smoke-filled airport, surrounded by abandoned Soviet military vehicles, and headed into the city. I didn't know anyone. I had $400 to last me three weeks. But there was something exciting about not knowing anyone in a new environment. I was alone, and yet I knew I was in the right place.

I learned that if you have faith enough to show up, shit happens. But how many people would get on an airplane with $400 and run off to an unknown country to start again? Not many, I assure you.

If you don't believe in your idea or yourself—I mean believe enough to bet the ranch and sacrifice precious time that can never be recaptured—don't do it. Leaders are believers, and people follow leaders. Businesses cannot be built without people, so you need to have that blind faith in what you are doing so you can share it. Without that kind of faith, no one is going help you on your journey. Faith is contagious.

Decide what you want, and believe you can have it. Even if it seems out of reach at the moment. Practice believing, be grateful, and move in the direction you want to go. You have a compass, so use it. It's your intuition. Life is a decision, and no one can make it but you. Ask yourself if you are willing to decide and have faith. Do you believe? Do you have enough faith to take a different path and get on with it? My wife likes to say you can't read the next chapter if you keep re-reading the last one. Faith gives me the courage to turn the page.

ACTIONS TO TAKE

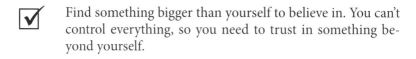 Find something bigger than yourself to believe in. You can't control everything, so you need to trust in something beyond yourself.

Don't worry about things you cannot control (which is mostly everything). Focus on your own responses.
Believe in yourself and the vision you have for your life. Have faith that you are where you're meant to be, and keep going. Faith protects you from the naysayers.

Show up and take that first leap forward. Sure, it's scary to step outside your comfort zone, to try to do what no one else is doing. But if you truly believe in your idea and yourself, you can do it—that's what makes you a leader.

Have faith and turn the next page in life. Leaders are believers, and that faith is contagious. Build your business with people who are inspired by your leadership and your blind faith in what you're doing.

My Notes

_____

_____

_____

_____

_____

_____

_____

_____

_____

_____

_____

_____

_____

_____

_____

_____

COMMITMENT

LEADERS COMMIT and make decisions. Don't listen to other people's opinions. Go with your intuition. Once I decided to stay in Estonia and rebuild my life, all kinds of doors opened up for me. I met people, and things happened; it was like I was just along for the ride.

William Hutchison Murray, a famous Scottish mountaineer, wrote a book called *The Scottish Himalayan Expedition.* The books starts:

> We had put down our passage money—booked a sailing to Bombay . . . until one is committed, there is hesitancy, the chance to draw back, always ineffectiveness. . . . Whatever you can do or dream, begin it. Boldness has genius, power and magic in it![i]

In the beginning, it takes me a long time to make a decision. I spend sleepless nights agitated and anxious. But when I determine my trajectory, the weight falls off my shoulders, and I wonder what all the fuss was about.

Entrepreneurs must make decisions and not look back. Once a commitment is made, I find it much easier to get on with whatever I'm meant to do. It's like trying to do a back dive off a high-dive board.

There's this massive swimming pool I used to go to. The water was always ice cold, and at the far end of the pool, you

---

i   Murray, William Hutchison. *The Scottish Himalayan Expedition.* London: J.M. Dent & Co., 1951. Pg. 7.

had to climb up stairs to get to a platform topped by a diving board. I'd watch for hours while young kids launched into all kinds of backflips and somersaults. It looked terrifying. How did they do that? Just run up there and flip backward?

One day I was with my son. I wanted to teach him not to be afraid of diving. He was four or five. He closely studied the other kids, and then he looked at me. I took his hand, and we climbed up the stairs to the platform. I knew I couldn't ask him to do something I couldn't do. I was afraid of diving boards and heights. As I looked down, my legs froze.

When I saw him looking at me, I made a decision not to let my fear dictate what I could do. I told him to watch; I explained to him I wasn't very good but that I would try anyway. And I did. It was fine. He happily jumped in after me. Once I made a commitment to my idea, my son followed. It works that way in business, too. When I committed to a plan, people came out of the woodwork to help and follow me.

HERE'S THE DEAL

After you decide, it's easy—but there is no turning back. A decision makes taking action much easier if you know it's final. The scary part of committing to anything is thinking about it. Stop thinking and take the plunge. Don't get me wrong—this is not easy, and I still look for all kinds of excuses to avoid decisions. But today, at least, I'm more capable of recognizing my procrastination, and I force myself to move forward. I've learned that nothing can stop me but my own thinking. As Nike says, "Just do it." What one thing have you been procrastinating about because you're afraid to face it or fearful of making a major mistake? Do you think you are able to do that one thing?

If you had to walk around the world, you could do it. How do you know? You know because once you take that first step, it's one step at a time, and eventually you'll arrive. You just need to take that first step and keep going, and each step becomes easier and easier.

ACTIONS TO TAKE

☑ Make a decision. Leaders must make tough choices. Get advice, but don't rely only on other people's opinions. Go with your intuition. Decide if this is what you want to do.

☑ Make a commitment to that decision. Entrepreneurs must make decisions and not look back; this frees you to move forward.

☑ Take a step. Stop thinking and take the plunge. Remember: a series of single steps is all it takes to eventually arrive at your goal. That first step can be hard, but they all get easier after that.

☑ Trust in the miracle. Once you've made your decision, committed to it, and taken the first step, you'll be amazed at how many doors open up for you. You'll never know until you try.

My Notes

Notes Contd.

_____

_____

_____

_____

_____

_____

_____

_____

_____

_____

_____

_____

_____

_____

_____

START LIFE AGAIN

NOW IS THE BEST TIME TO START. Not tomorrow or next week. Don't procrastinate. It's tempting to want to have everything perfect before you launch into something new. It's also a great excuse to never get started. It saves us from trying and failing. It protects our sensitive egos. Fear of failure, embarrassment, ridicule, or being lost scares most of us.

Didn't we grow up believing we had to do things correctly? Even in school, our teachers graded our exams by marking whether we'd answered the questions correctly or not. Our mindsets are focused on knowing all the answers before venturing out. At least that was the way I used to think. The bottom line is that we are afraid to make mistakes so we don't push the boundaries and try.

It always starts with a step. That's it. Only a step. Just like my first dive off the diving board, your venture doesn't need to be perfect at the start. That will come with time.

This past year, I got a message on LinkedIn from a young Nigerian living in London. He had started a business in England using African products, and he had read about me somewhere and wanted to connect. His name was Tula. I accepted his LinkedIn invitation and thought nothing more about it. A few days later, I got an email message asking if I'd meet with him. He explained how he had decided to start his business and how he needed advice. Normally, I don't meet total strangers in cafés, but something about his business description intrigued me: I wanted to learn more. So I met with him.

We met in London in a café on Sloan Square. The same café where I used to take my son and wife to breakfast on the school run in the morning. Today it's one of my favorite short business meeting places—it sure does serve the best eggs. But the day I met with Tula led to the idea for this book and more. I'll get back to that story in a minute.

HERE'S THE DEAL

My guess is that if you have a business idea or are thinking of quitting your job and setting out on your own, you are hesitant. Of course you are; you are afraid it won't work. Afraid you are not ready. You don't have all the information. You don't have all the answers and need more time. I think that's how most of us operate. We all hate the unknown, and we would rather not take any chances and let things carry on as they are. The thing is, since most people think that way, anyone who thinks differently and just tries begins with a distinct advantage. They are far down the road before anyone else gives it a go.

In *A More Beautiful Question*, Warren Berger talks about an interesting experiment measuring a group of kindergarten children against Harvard MBA students. The groups were divided and given spaghetti, string, tape, and a marshmallow and told to assemble the tallest structure they could in fifteen minutes. The outcome is probably no surprise. The grads spent too much time arguing about the project and who would be in charge. Meanwhile, the children jumped right in and worked, adapting quickly to successes and failures. As Berger says, "The point of the marshmallow experiment was not to humble MBA students (if anything, that was a side benefit), but rather to better understand how to make progress when tasked with a difficult challenge in uncertain conditions."[ii] What we learn from this is the power of just cracking on and trying things quickly to see what works and what doesn't.

In my first few months in Estonia, I saved enough money to move into my first office. There was only my assistant and me. It wasn't much. No name on the door, no fancy furniture. It was a blank canvas. In the beginning, it's easy to make mistakes: they don't cost much. Ultimately, in those early stages, it's easy to shut down the whole thing if it doesn't work. Once your model is proven and working, then blast out. But in the beginning, start small and stay away from big markets. The key is to start; don't worry if you don't have all the answers.

Learn as you build. If you're wrong, you can make adjustments and get the model right. Starting small means you are flexible, and there is little to lose. You can always start over again like the kids did with their spaghetti-and-marshmallow structure. Don't overthink things.

When I started my first company, I had three people on my team. We had no idea what we were doing, and everyone in the market ignored us. We borrowed an office from a friend, and we asked for favors. Back then, I was renovating apartments and selling them. At any given moment, I could have folded the tent and moved on. We were testing the market. We were trying. Eventually, we had to add on operations: bookkeepers, accountants, and a marketing and sales staff. By 2006, my agency business was a team of 350 employees in thirty-five offices across Central and Eastern Europe. Like those kids in

---

ii   Berger, Warren. *A More Beautiful Question: The Power of Inquiry to Spark Breakthrough Ideas.* Bloomsbury: New York, 2014. Pg. 121.

the spaghetti experiment, we just cracked on, and every time we hit a roadblock, we went another way. But we kept on.

ACTIONS TO TAKE

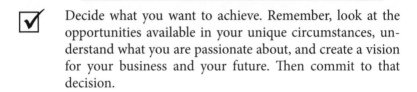

☑ Decide what you want to achieve. Remember, look at the opportunities available in your unique circumstances, understand what you are passionate about, and create a vision for your business and your future. Then commit to that decision.

☑ Pick one thing and do that. It always starts with a step. That's it. Only a step.

☑ Start now. Don't hesitate. Of course, you are afraid you are not ready, afraid you don't have all the answers, and afraid of the unknown. Most people are afraid of those same things, so if you have the courage to start now, you begin with a distinct advantage.

☑ Do it quickly. There is power in just cracking on and trying things to see what works and what doesn't. If it doesn't work or you make a mistake, try something new. Learn as you build. When you're wrong, make adjustments until you get the model right.

My Notes

Notes Contd.

_____

_____

_____

_____

_____

_____

_____

_____

_____

_____

_____

_____

_____

_____

_____

_____

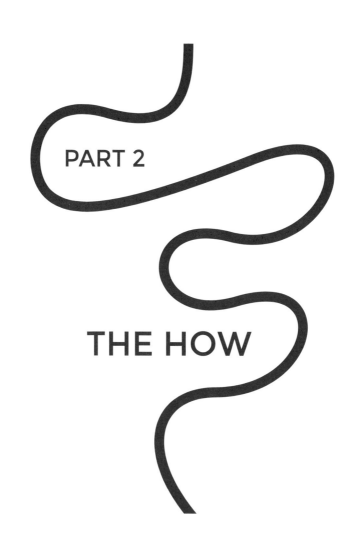

PART 2

THE HOW

MAKE "YOUR" THING "THEIR" THING

REMEMBER THAT TULA AND I met in the Sloan Square café? Well, my meeting with the young Nigerian left me intrigued, and I started researching Africa and his product idea. I jotted ideas down and made lists. My new friend was struggling, and he had done just about everything wrong he could possibly do. But I liked his brand, and I liked his idea. I decided to look into it more closely. I walked down to Ryman's office and stationery store on King's Road in Chelsea and purchased a notebook for my African business ideas.

When I was writing admissions essays for business school about what I wanted to do, I didn't realize that all the things I was writing about would come true. Writing and storytelling are powerful tools and key skills for anyone who wants to build a company. Entrepreneurs become great by inspiring customers and their team with a vision. They become great storytellers and share their passion for their vision. Their excitement is contagious, and they attract good people who will follow them.

I think a lot of people may feel silly writing out stuff in grandiose ways, cutting out pictures and mapping things out that don't exist yet. It all may feel a bit fantastic. But I assure you, it works. And history from the beginning of time proves this.

Writing ideas down may be the most powerful tool of all. I try not to talk about any of my ideas until I'm ready. Writing is action, and it takes the idea from your mind to the paper. It sounds easy, but it isn't. Next time you have an amazing idea, try writing it down, and you will find that it's not easy at all. Most people don't do it properly, or they simply give up.

Once you start to write, all kinds of things happen. When you finally do manage to get it the way you want it on paper, your brain has gone through an amazing process. Your plan will remain in your subconscious, and while you're not looking, it will find a way to manifest itself. Jung called this "synchronicity"; I call it having my prayers answered—when events coincide with what I have mapped out in my mind. Putting those ideas on paper says to God or the Universe that you're ready. When you write, you will be one of the few people who actually takes that critical step, and this will be to your advantage.

HERE'S THE DEAL

Most people just talk about things. You know the type. They sit behind a bar and dazzle people with their great ideas. They are great at dinner parties, sharing what they are going to do. But very few of those people take the time to sit down, pen in hand, sketch it out, and try it. If you can write down your plan, create a story, and simplify and streamline what's in your head, you are more than halfway there. Then all you need to do is give it a try.

Imagine you are an architect. Every architect needs a plan. You can't construct a building without one. Everyone knows this, so why do so few draft a plan for their business or their life? Early on, I cut out pictures and put them on a board to look at every day. It was my storyboard. Build a business plan, no matter how basic. Your plan will grow and evolve once you start. But never stop writing your plan. It should grow as you grow and change as your business changes.

Like most successful businesses, my business started as something I did on the side. In 1993, I was helping a friend I'd made in Estonia build up the credit department at his bank. At the same time, I started renovating apartments and renting them out to embassy personnel. A year later, when I left the bank, I'd flipped about five apartments. I was using a host of people at different real estate agencies to find inventory for me, and I asked a few if they wanted to work with me full time. That was the start of our retail agency business.

Did you know that a pilot flying a plane is almost always off course? A plane spends 95 percent of its flight off its charted course. Weather, wind, and a variety of other factors shift an airplane from its intended flight plan. So pilots often reevaluate their position and make corrections to ultimately land exactly on target. Why don't we do that with our lives?

Like that pilot, you need to course correct. When you write something down over and over, it gets clarified. You create a powerful tool to make your goals come true. But like anything, you will need to constantly revise as your circumstances change.

ACTIONS TO TAKE

☑ Dare to have dreams. Don't be afraid to have a big goal. Far more is possible than you've let yourself dream.

☑ Sketch out a draft version of your goals. Writing and storytelling are powerful tools for anyone who wants to build a company.

☑ Simplify it so that you can explain it easily to others. Effectively sharing your dream with other people is critical to building the right team of employees, investors, and consultants.

☑ Write it out again, and use pictures. This may feel silly at times, but it truly is important!

☑ Let go and let it happen. Once you start to write, all kinds of things happen. When you finally manage to get it the way you want it on paper, your brain has gone through an amazing process.

☑ Be flexible and keep rewriting. When you write something down over and over, it gets clarified. You create a powerful tool to make your goals come true. But you will need to constantly revise as circumstances change.

My Notes

_____

_____

_____

_____

_____

_____

_____

_____

_____

_____

_____

_____

_____

_____

_____

_____

_____

Notes Contd.

_____

_____

_____

_____

_____

_____

_____

_____

_____

_____

_____

_____

_____

_____

_____

_____

HELP

A S KIDS, WE ARE PROGRAMMED to think that there is a right way and a wrong way to do things. But sometimes we don't want to appear stupid, so we don't ask for help.

Ask for help. It's the single most important thing you can learn to do in life. Most people love helping others. People especially tend to help those who are more successful than they are. Ask for directions; don't keep driving around the block looking for the gas station like your dad did. It will drive everyone around you nuts.

My new Nigerian friend Tula needed help. He reached out and contacted me directly. Even as a complete stranger, I could relate to what he was going through and wanted to be helpful, so I met with him a few more times, trying to guide him to the right professionals. What I discovered was that he had surrounded himself with people who wanted to take advantage of him. Now his company was in debt, and these people were chasing him. They wanted their money back. In desperation, and as a last resort, he was looking for me to bail him out and lend him money. He needed my help, but he didn't need a handout. That was the worst thing I could have done for him. I could help Tula, as I'll talk about in the next chapter, but not by giving him a loan with his current business structure.

I needed help when I first started Ober-Haus, my real estate company. I hired people who were all smarter than I was. I was the guy with the idea, but I knew very little about the market and how things worked. I found most people were happy to help me and give me advice. I spoke with a lot of professionals, and even though sometimes my inexperience made me seem stupid, I found that it was a blessing in disguise.

Because I worked in countries where I didn't speak the language, I was forced to hire people to do many things. Most first-time entrepreneurs like to do everything themselves, but to be successful, you need to have others do things for you. You need to delegate so you can lead—others will manage, and others will do the day-to-day work.

Out of necessity, I learned to ask people to help me, and that allowed me the freedom to grow my vision and do many more things I was good at—like creating new businesses.

HERE'S THE DEAL

Not knowing something means you have to start at the beginning. That's a good thing. Not knowing forces you to ask questions. You don't need to have the answers to get started, just the questions. Then find people who know the answers, and hire them.

When I started helping my friend at the bank build his credit department, I knew nothing about banking. I asked for help. When I started building apartments, I had never built anything before, so I hired builders who had. When I started my retail real estate agency business, I knew nothing about real estate services, so I hired people from other agencies. I knew what I wanted; I just didn't know how to do those things.

As a leader, if you have a vision and can tell your story well and inspire people, finding people to execute your vision will not be a problem. They will flock to you. Your job is knowing what the questions are; their job is providing the answers.

Also, who do you talk to about things that aren't working or concerns you have? You can't really confide your fears to your employees—that only backfires. You don't want your team to know you are unsure or concerned. So you need a group, or at least several individuals, that you can talk to on a regular basis. This may mean developing a good relationship with your lawyer or your corporate finance guy if you're working with one. If you have investors, they are also a good sounding board to bounce ideas off of. Naturally, they want you to succeed, so they make themselves available for the important discussions.

But beyond that, I suggest getting involved with local mastermind groups and joining forums of like-minded people. The internet is full of chat groups and forums that discuss specific topics—some are free and some cost. These are professional groups of business owners and entrepreneurs that all have the same issues you do, and they provide both a vital source of information and a shoulder to cry on. I know some people who have been going to the same groups for years, and they find it a huge help in overcoming business obstacles, and even personal issues, that they face as entrepreneurs.

ACTIONS TO TAKE

☑ Pinpoint what you need to know. There will be many things you need to know that you don't know. This is not a problem. You can't do everything yourself, and you can't be the best at everything. You need outside wisdom.

☑ Don't ask for handouts. If your business is failing, a handout won't help you.

☑ Do ask for advice. Your job is knowing what questions to ask and finding people who know the answers.

☑ Hire professionals who know what you need to know. Most first-time entrepreneurs like to do everything themselves, but to be successful, you need to have others do things for you. You need to delegate.

☑ Join a forum of like-minded business people or a mastermind group. Use this support system to gain and share knowledge and encouragement with other professionals who are walking the same path.

My Notes

Notes Contd.

_____

_____

_____

_____

_____

_____

_____

_____

_____

_____

_____

_____

_____

_____

_____

BUILD A GREAT TEAM

YOU DON'T FLY to the moon alone, my wife likes to remind me. She reminds me a lot because I need to hear it. Entrepreneurs need a ground team. You cannot mentally and physically do everything alone, even though sometimes I like to think I can do it all by myself.

My new friend Tula had tried to build his company by himself. He didn't have a team, just a group of people that had lent him money and now wanted it back. It was too late for him to restructure his business: it was too far gone. I introduced him to a friend of mine who is an insolvency professional and could help him manage his debt. He told Tula to fire his accountant— an uncle he disliked who was also chasing him for money—and to slowly gather people around him who could help him.

I knew the pain he felt. I was there many years ago when I started a company in Norwalk, Connecticut. We grew fast and built up a team in the direct marketing business. We had a warehouse full of product and an office full of women answering phones. Then we lost our single contract. It was painful. I had people chasing me for money, suppliers threatening me, and the government looking for taxes. It's a lonely place, and suddenly you realize you don't have many friends. Like Tula, I wanted to be bailed out. That wasn't going to happen, and I had to learn that the hard way. In hindsight, it taught me some valuable lessons.

To succeed at anything, you need a team behind you, carrying out your visions and plans and executing the work. But let's be clear on one thing: leadership is not management. You are not a manager—you are an entrepreneur, and there is a difference between the two. I had to learn how to delegate, mostly out of necessity. It was a blessing in disguise because it forced me to rely on others.

At Ober-Haus, we did everything together—celebrated, had birthday parties in our offices, and went on weekends away. We hung out in saunas and jumped into freezing lakes together. We had awards parties where we gave out trophies for the best salesperson and best employee, along with prizes for some goofy things as well. Everyone loved it. We did everything we could together, and over time, we all became one big family.

In eighteen years of business with some 850 employees, I only lost five in total and only two that I had to fire.

Your team should be people you like. And they should have skills you don't have, which if you're like me, means pretty much everything. You will know quickly if they blend in with others or if they're difficult. If they don't fit in, let them go, and find new people. Keep doing that until you put together the right team. I say this because you will spend a lot of your time with these people. You want your team to not watch the clock but to work hard and follow you. You will probably spend more time with them than with your family. So finding the right team is crucial to your success.

HERE'S THE DEAL

When I started my first business in Estonia in 1992, my team consisted of my personal assistant, who was also my translator, and me. We really weren't doing anything extraordinary. We were just learning and trying stuff out.

At meetings, someone would start speaking in Estonian, and I wouldn't have a clue what they'd said until my assistant translated for me. I was on the back foot from the very start. So for me, hiring people became a necessity. It wasn't a strategy about building a great internal team; it was about being able to function as best as I could. So instead of being involved in every aspect of the business, I learned to hire people to do things. Then, to keep myself current, I met with these people (my managers) on a regular basis each week.

Besides your internal team, you need to build a team outside the company. Some people call this networking. I see these people as an extension of my business. These people are just as important as your internal team, and in some critical moments, even more important. The lawyers, architects, marketing and PR specialists, accountants, and construction companies we worked with—these were my outside team members. I made sure I hired the best, and I had a lot of them on retainer. As an entrepreneur, you need to network. You never know when all these people will come in handy.

In 1998, during the Russian currency crisis, the banks suddenly stopped lending, and I was right in the middle of an important big-box retail development for a German retailer. I was ten million euros from completion. The banks wanted more equity, and we didn't have it. I was in trouble. I asked for help. My go-to construction company had built four large retail centers for me in the past, and they had cash and resources. They financed me out of my predicament until I completed the project and could finally back-end the financing with the banks. You never know when your team will really bail you out.

ACTIONS TO TAKE

☑ Recognize you don't fly to the moon alone. Entrepreneurs, like astronauts, need a ground team. You cannot mentally or physically do everything yourself.

☑ Look at your business and ask yourself what its most important components are. Pretend you know nothing (even if you do) and identify jobs to fill. You need key employees managing each of those areas, carrying out your vision and plans, and executing the work.

☑ Find the right people to support you in each discipline—both with your internal team and through a network of companies and professionals. Your team should be people you like. And they should have skills you don't have.

☑ Reward your team and build camaraderie through work and play. Retaining your team is crucial for success.

My Notes

Notes Contd.

_____

_____

_____

_____

_____

_____

_____

_____

_____

_____

_____

_____

_____

_____

_____

_____

LEAD, DON'T MANAGE

DON'T COMPARE apples to oranges. Entrepreneurs are not managers. You don't want to be both, and you cannot be both if you want your business to succeed. So many people get this all confused, and I think it's a fundamental problem when starting, growing, and running a business. An entrepreneur is someone who develops a vision, knows the endgame, and shares that vision with his team, investors, bankers, and customers. Entrepreneurs create change; managers make sure the change happens. It is impossible to do both well.

When I was building a business in Central and Eastern Europe, I was a leader, not a manager. There was so much I didn't know how to do, but I did know how to create interest around an idea, sell that idea, and build great teams.

Management and leadership are both important; in fact, they go hand in hand. But they are two separate functions, carried out by different people. In a business, there should be one leader, many managers, and a healthy team. They will work 24/7 for you if they believe in and trust you. No, we don't fly to the moon alone. We need help. Without loyal troops, leaders would be incapable.

Managers implement systems. They execute and try to improve efficiency in service and production. Good managers get the most out of people and processes. Managers make your life easy. You give them the plan. They make it happen. Entrepreneurs design. Managers build.

I'll give you an example. I hate to travel. I like being in my own bed at night, reading my books, writing, making lists, and thinking. When I travel, I feel unsettled and transient. I don't think well, and I feel tired.

So when we expanded our business to other countries, I looked for a young guy who loved to travel and liked going out to dinners and discovering new nightclubs. And I found him. That guy opened all my offices in five countries. He was always on the road, and he loved it. On my own, I could never have done what he did. I didn't have that skill set. The good news was that I knew that.

HERE'S THE DEAL

As a leader, I'm good at finding the right people to do the job. I know what the picture is meant to look like and where I want to get to, but I couldn't tell you how to mix concrete or service a hotel. That's not my job, and I hate details. I can do details, but I'm terrible at them.

Years later, when I found myself turning around a country house hotel that I had purchased, I had to do details. Funds were low. I was in trouble, and I couldn't afford to bring in people to help me. I knew I'd be forcing myself to manage operations. I'm not made for that, and while I knew I could do it, I also knew I wouldn't do the best job of it. Eventually, I would need to bring in managers if I wanted to survive. Managers are specialists, and leaders are generalists—we're not wired for details.

Finally, after months of doing a lot of things I really disliked, I started bringing in the help I needed, and that made all the difference. Before that, my wife would say, "Just teach him to do what you would do," or "Show her how to be more organized." All very easy to say, but it's like asking a duck to ice skate. Every day, I'd go and do my job, and I was miserable. I was a terrible manager. I knew I was wasting my time. I'd spend half the day thinking up ideas, when I really needed to be working in operations.

When I invested in a fast food chain years later, I witnessed the same dynamic at work. The owner would try to be helpful by running the register if the store was too busy, making purchases, working on menus, doing the marketing, working on fit-out with designers and architects, and trying to find new locations. Very impressive, but not the way to grow a business. We changed all that, and the business grew.

As a business owner, chances are you are a leader. Remember, it's your idea, your vision, and your company. Lead. Don't manage.

ACTIONS TO TAKE

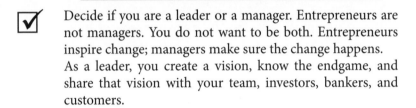 Decide if you are a leader or a manager. Entrepreneurs are not managers. You do not want to be both. Entrepreneurs inspire change; managers make sure the change happens.
As a leader, you create a vision, know the endgame, and share that vision with your team, investors, bankers, and customers.

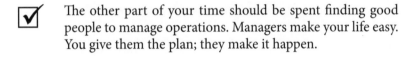 The other part of your time should be spent finding good people to manage operations. Managers make your life easy. You give them the plan; they make it happen.

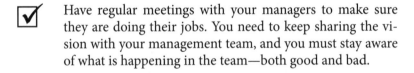 Have regular meetings with your managers to make sure they are doing their jobs. You need to keep sharing the vision with your management team, and you must stay aware of what is happening in the team—both good and bad.

My Notes

Notes Contd.

_____

_____

_____

_____

_____

_____

_____

_____

_____

_____

_____

_____

_____

_____

_____

_____

IDEAS

I **HAVE TWENTY IDEAS A DAY.** Twenty great ideas! They come and go. Ideas are perishable. They come in a blink of an eye, like a eureka moment, and they hit us without warning. A half hour later, I've forgotten them.

Most of my ideas are great, and so are yours. But probably, like mine, your ideas are usually impractical. One day, I may have an amazing idea about international money transfers, and the next day I'll envision how to do stocktaking for a fast food chain. But if I'm not in those sectors already, chances are it will be extremely difficult for me to get any traction without investing significant time and resources. I'm not saying it can't be done, but it's a long shot.

As we discussed earlier, ask yourself, "Where are you?" Look at your unique circumstances and what you're doing right now. You really can't get to point B if you don't know where A is. And you don't need to know *how* to get from where you are to point B right away. You just need to have a grasp of the general direction you need to go.

As I helped Tula liquidate his company, I also started researching Africa. Strangely, it seemed like every Facebook and LinkedIn post I was reading featured startups in Africa, entrepreneurship, and team building. I also started following people on LinkedIn and Twitter and paying attention to the current news in the region. One day I read an article written by an entrepreneur and startup thought leader named John-Paul Iwuoha. He had written a book, *101 Ways to Make Money in Africa*, which was full of thought-provoking business ideas. He had founded a company called Small Starters and was doing a lot of blogging on entrepreneurship. So I started following him and sent him an invitation to connect. Then I waited.

HERE'S THE DEAL

Back in the 1980s, when I was about eighteen years old, my trading buddy and I would go down to the deli for coffee, and every morning we would get our hot coffee in those Greek-style paper coffee cups with the plastic lid on top. One day, my friend ripped a v-shaped hole in the plastic top of the coffee lid so he could both cool it and drink it while keeping the lid on. Suddenly, we both looked at each other and had a eureka moment. "Hey, wouldn't it be cool if all plastic lids had a flip-top?" we said.

Well, we all know the rest of the story. We were eighteen-year-olds with no money. We'd never invented anything, and we were clerks on the trading floor. We didn't do anything with the idea. Today, of course, every plastic lid has a perforated hole. Great idea.

Yes, I wish I'd invented the flip-top lid, video real estate, colored flip-flops, and about a hundred other great ideas I've had over the years. Really, I could have made a billion dollars. But ideas are universal. I've got a hunch that every time we have an idea, someone else in the world is having the same thought. Circumstances determine who makes it work and who has the ability to move forward with that idea at any given moment. Don't feel bad about it. One day you will grab the right idea that fits the place you're at, and you won't even know it's coming.

Back in Estonia, one day I was writing business plans for Sergei, and the next thing I knew, I was working in a new bank—and then after that, I started buying and flipping apartments. Those dots connected in ways I never would have imagined. In hindsight, it looks like A to Z, but actually, I was jumping all over the map. One day, one of my employees walked into my office and laid a map out on the table. "Here," he said, "is where we should build a grocery store." And that was really the beginning of the shopping centers we built for the next fifteen years. One day before, I would have never imagined building shopping centers. I mean, for real?

Strangely, each of these ideas snuck up on me, slowly developing in their own magic way, until suddenly there was a confluence into one Big Idea.

When I started building shopping centers, I was already in the real estate business. I was doing something I knew about and had already been drawn to. I wasn't suddenly designing women's fashion accessories. If you start with one thing, it will eventually take you down the right path without you noticing. Chances are the business you want to start or are involved in right now is related to something you know about, or are passionate about, or have been thinking about for some time. Steve Jobs studied graphics and design; he didn't go into fast food. When you take strides toward your vision, you'll come to know your arena pretty well.

Once you've committed mentally and thought about how to proceed, you need to start committing in a real way. Take your idea and make a storyboard, a plan: Who do you know who can help you? What should you do first? What kind of budget do you have? Blast all this stuff down on paper, and more ideas will flow. Get it out of your head. What does it look like? If you don't like it, start again. Write down everything. Make a shopping list of things you will need, starting from day one.

ACTIONS TO TAKE

☑ Make a habit of brainstorming, and let your ideas flow. You'll have many crazy or impractical ideas, but the perfect idea will strike at just the right time.

☑ Find what you enjoy doing or what you see yourself doing. Remember that the golden idea is almost always one that fits with your skills or what you've always dreamed of doing. Catch the idea that represents who you are.

☑ Consider your circumstances. Remember that steps toward your vision are a confluence of your ideas and your circumstances; one day you will grab the right idea that fits the place you're at.

My Notes

_____

_____

_____

_____

_____

_____

_____

_____

_____

_____

_____

_____

_____

_____

_____

_____

Notes Contd.

_____

_____

_____

_____

_____

_____

_____

_____

_____

_____

_____

_____

_____

_____

_____

_____

GET GOOD AT EXECUTION

I BOUGHT John-Paul's book about African business ideas, and four days after I sent him a LinkedIn invitation, I saw he had "liked" one of my posts. The next day he connected with me. I sent him an email. We exchanged a few messages about business, and I gradually introduced myself; he did the same. I read his blogs, and he read mine. I thought it might be a good idea to meet, maybe in London. I messaged him about Tula and his story. I wasn't sure where any of this was really going, but I was drawn to it. I felt it was going somewhere, and I wanted to let it happen. We agreed a meeting would be good, but he told me he was living in Lagos. We decided to Skype instead. That's the power of technology.

In a matter of weeks, I'd moved from a chance meeting to reading a blog on LinkedIn to sending a message to Lagos to Skyping a new friend across the ocean.

Ultimately, the key is not the million-dollar idea but the million-dollar execution. Personally, I'll always take a mediocre idea that I know something about and can execute well over a great idea that I know nothing about and will execute poorly. The execution is the single most important aspect of success in any business. As a leader, you need to hire managers who can execute your ideas and ensure they get the job done. Steve Wozniak knew about computers; Steve Jobs didn't. Apple was only possible with both of their skill sets.

You can spend all the money and time you want on marketing and sales, building your digital platform, and public relations, but if the machinery isn't working properly, if you aren't paying attention to execution, you might as well just close the door and go fishing. It's all a waste of money unless you can deliver.

Once my consultant repeatedly tried to call me at my office at a hotel I owned. Finally, she emailed me: "No one is answering the phone—call me."

I walked out of the building and into the main house. I wandered down the medieval corridor of my hotel, a fantastic Tudor-period building with twelve acres of beautiful topiary gardens. But it was strangely empty. I saw no waiters. I kept walking. When I reached the front desk, no one was there. The phone was ringing. I'd just spent thousands of UK pounds boosting ads on Facebook, writing blogs, and sending e-shots. Yet the cold reality was that the phone was ringing, and no one was answering. That is bad execution. Clearly my fault.

HERE'S THE DEAL

I've owned four hotels and had one that only made it to the planning stage. They dotted Central and Eastern Europe and were the first luxury, five-star hotels in some of those cities. We were some of the first entrepreneurs in the desert of what was the former Soviet Union, so people came to us in droves. Anyone who was anyone stayed with us. They came because we offered something different: service and luxury in a market that was lacking both.

I was fortunate enough to hire German and Austrian hotel managers who knew their stuff, and they put an eager group of locals through the paces of customer service and operations. Our local team was excited and willing to work hard. Because they were thrilled to have jobs at such prestigious hotels, they never watched the clock. This was an opportunity for them. They were proud of their jobs, and they cared about what the customers thought.

Years later, I tried the same experiment and bought a country house hotel in the UK. But the difference in the staff I hired was clear from day one—no one wanted to work. No one cared about service or quality; most people were only interested in their paycheck, and everyone watched the clock. It took restarting with a whole new staff, including many young Spanish employees who really wanted their jobs and were willing to work hard. I've had nineteen restaurants in London, and the story was the same. Every time I hired staff who watched the clock, things floundered, but every time my employees were determined to succeed, the enterprise proved successful.

Since execution is the single most important ingredient for success, you better make sure you have the staff to make it happen. Hire people who want to work, and reward them. Create a vertical ladder of opportunities for your employees, and train them relentlessly. If you don't know how, bring in someone who does.

Think of all the businesses you know of. Most are in crowded sectors. What makes the good ones stand out over the others? Execution. A lot of other factors come into play, but fundamentally, it all boils down to execution.

If your employees aren't getting the job done, fire them. Don't be trapped by personalities and loyalty. Give a new employee a thorough try, of course. Start by being specific about what they need to do. If they struggle to do their job well because they simply don't know what they're doing wrong, bring in someone to help them. If that fails, there is only the door. You'd be surprised how many entrepreneurs get tied to ineffective staff because they like them or feel bad about firing someone. I've done it myself many times, and I only have myself to blame for the shabby results. You're in business to create, build, and add value. Don't waste your time. Answer the friggin' phone, and only keep staff members who are determined to work hard and care about success.

ACTIONS TO TAKE

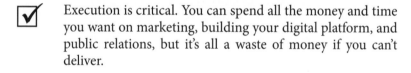 Execution is critical. You can spend all the money and time you want on marketing, building your digital platform, and public relations, but it's all a waste of money if you can't deliver.

Only hire staff members who are eager and willing to work hard. Then pay them well and earn their loyalty.

Train your employees, and give them the tools for success. Good employees and managers are determined to succeed. Encourage that determination by creating a vertical ladder of opportunities.

If employees don't want to work or don't care about service or quality, let them go. Since execution is the single most important ingredient to success, you have to ensure your staff is willing to make that happen.

My Notes

Notes Contd.

_____

_____

_____

_____

_____

_____

_____

_____

_____

_____

_____

_____

_____

_____

OWNERSHIP

TULA WAS FACING a problem familiar to many entrepreneurs. In his quest to raise capital for his new venture, he had relied on friends, family, and casual acquaintances. Most people think this is the logical place to start. It's not.

He did not control his business: his friends and family did. And because of his relationships with them, making tough decisions became even more difficult. When you start losing your family's money, it's not easy to sit at the dinner table with them. There is either uncomfortable silence or a lot of arguing. Either way, not good.

The same thing happens when you share ownership with a partner. Yes, maybe your friend is a great guy, or maybe you just want a partner, but when things go wrong or tough decisions need to be made, you need to be able to act quickly and execute change without lengthy discussions. Having an equal partner on the ground will cripple your ability to do that. Partnerships always struggle with deadlock. Don't partner, and don't do business with friends you want to keep. You need to own as much of the company's equity as possible so that there are no arguments.

Recently I invested in a fast food chain in London. It was trendsetting, and I wanted in. I was excited, and I needed a new project. "This is it!" I thought. I found the young owner, and we struck a deal. It was fifty-fifty; we were partners joined at the hip. It was a happy day, but our euphoria lasted for only that day.

HERE'S THE DEAL

My partner had started the fast food company and had always run the show. I had always been the majority owner and run my own companies when I was in Central and Eastern Europe. My outside institutional investors let me get on with things. Outside of the occasional phone call and financial report, I hardly ever saw them. But when I signed the deal with my new fast food partner, I was entering into something completely different. Now I was the investor, but I had always been an operator. So when I showed up for work the following day, our relationship became a battle—a push-and-pull struggle.

Another time, a good friend and I decided to buy a business together. We were equal partners. Everything went great in the beginning, but when more money was required, my friend was unwilling to invest more heavily in the business, nor did he want to dilute his shareholding by allowing me to invest more on my own. We found ourselves in a deadlock. He screamed "fuck you" at me several times in a row, and working with him became untenable. Our friendship, whatever it had been, was over.

I'd known this guy eighteen years. We'd had dozens of dinners and gone on vacation together. He sent me tickets to football games. He wasn't my best buddy, but he was a buddy and someone I liked and respected.

Falling out with him over a business deal killed our friendship. Today, I have to ask, "Why?" What was a more valuable asset in the long run—the business or our friendship? That's a decision you never want to force yourself into having to make. In a partnership, there are two leaders, and each eventually develops a different agenda. That will never work long term. As a leader, you need to be singular. Always own the majority of shares.

But you will need capital to grow. So who do you ask? Where do you go when you need capital? How do you maintain control? How do you keep the majority of the shares? That's an entirely different kettle of fish. Your business will grow, and you will need money, which you'll get through equity and bank debt. Diluting your share of equity is often unavoidable, so you'll give some to incoming investors. You will probably need the cash to grow or to get out of trouble.

There's a big distinction between a private equity investor or a professional investor and your friend or relative who's ready to be your partner. Professional or institutional investors are too busy doing deals, raising capital, and monitoring their investments for exit to want to sit next to you at your desk and question your decisions. They are busy. That's not their job.

When I was a young stockbroker, I felt guilty when I lost money for the doctors or dentists that were my clients. I couldn't sleep at night. However, if I lost money for an institutional investor, I wasn't distressed. I didn't like having lost money, but I realized these were professional investors; they'd already underwritten a portion of their portfolios to loss. It wasn't a personal thing. Food wouldn't come off their tables. Whereas if I helped a friend or family member invest a portion of his savings, it did hurt him if he lost—and by extension, it hurt me. That's the difference between family investors and professional investors.

Also, keep in mind that even if you need to give a majority

of your shares to private equity investors at the beginning, there will be ways to maintain control and claw back your equity. As the operating partner, you will always have control over business operations (unless you really screw up), and based on performance, you will be able to earn back more equity as your business grows.

Finally, don't exclude debt as an option. Debt by its very nature is cheaper than equity. Simplistically, debt has a rate of interest, and you need to pay it back at some point. Interest payments can be a drain on cash flow if there is too much debt, but I'd rather pay a bank interest than give a majority of my shares away any day.

Equity is the dearest thing, and it's expensive. Don't give it away; don't share it if you don't have to, especially with friends and relatives. These are people you need to see every day and eat Christmas dinner with. Go watch a football game with them, and get money from the professionals.

ACTIONS TO TAKE

☑ Control your own business. As a leader, you need to be singular: own the majority of the shares. When tough decisions need to be made, you need to be able to execute without lengthy discussions.

☑ When you need more capital, be clear about how much money you need now and, if possible, over the next five years.

☑ Don't partner or do business with friends you want to keep. Falling out over business deals or debt kills friendships.
Start talking to professional investors. Consider what professional investors bring to the table beyond equity—like experience, wise counsel, and connections with other experts. Don't exclude debt as an option. Go talk to your bank. Ask if they have a business-growth lending department. Interest payments can be a drain on cash flow if there is too much debt, but it's usually better than selling a majority of your shares.

☑ Decide if you want to raise money with debt or equity (or a mixture of both). Hire a good corporate lawyer to draft any agreements.

My Notes

_____

_____

_____

_____

_____

_____

_____

_____

_____

_____

_____

_____

_____

_____

_____

_____

_____

LEARN TO COUNT

RECENTLY, I spoke at an entrepreneur conference at a well-known business school in Oxford. The room was full of experienced executives who were taking an entrepreneurial course for a week. They were looking to start their own businesses. It was a well-heeled crowd. I was only one of many speakers throughout the week, and my talk told the story of how I'd grown my businesses in such a short period of time. We talked about faith, ideas, building a team, networking, and branding. Before wrapping up with exit strategies, I paused to touch base on accounting. I wasn't planning on spending too much time on it.

I asked how many people did their own personal accounting every month: reviewing their assets, debt, and personal cash flows. I have always done my own, and for the last twenty-eight years I've accounted for every penny. I think if you do this for yourself, it becomes easier to manage the business end of accounting. Out of a group of thirty-five adult business people, only two raised their hands. I found this incredible. I was standing in front of a group of executives who never did their own accounting. Yes, they paid the bills each month, and maybe based expenses on their bank balance and had a sketchy idea of their future budget—but that was it.

I look at my personal records every week and do monthly accounts. It keeps me focused and helps me make wise decisions. I can't imagine how to do it any other way. Especially as your business grows—you acquire assets and toys, repay debt, plan vacations, and deal with unexpected events. What if things slow down, and your business goes bust or cannot support you anymore? You can't afford to be blindsided by bad news. I'm a big believer in planning ahead.

The last time I met with Tula, I asked him to bring his accounts. Before he liquidated his company, I wanted to see how bad its future really looked. I was looking to see what assets were in his operating company and what he could salvage. Did he have any patents or trademark rights? What was his goodwill worth?

Sadly there wasn't much there, and he wasn't able to explain any of it to me because the figures had been done by someone else—his uncle. He didn't understand the burn rate of cash he was going through. All he knew was that he was out of money, yet he was still producing and creating more supplier debt.

HERE'S THE DEAL

In my first year of recovery back in 1987, I was confronted with the harsh reality of the mess I'd made of my life and the amount of money I'd actually wasted. Receiving a fat paycheck every two weeks from the trading company where I worked allowed me to be reckless with dinners and nightclubs. That meant, of course, that I was always out having too much fun and not being a responsible adult. The tidal wave of debt hit me hard.

I used to shove my bills into a shoebox. That was the level of my administrative abilities. I figured that if I didn't see them, I could forget about them. Occasionally I'd get phone calls, and

I'd send off a check in the mail. Pretty soon, I stopped taking calls, just like Tula was doing now.

One day I was introduced to a book written by a guy named Jerrold Mundis.[iii] It was about spending plans and how to get out of debt. My girlfriend (who later became my wife) gave me the book when she discovered my bill shoebox. That's when everything changed for me.

I blew through the book, and within a month, I worked out payment plans with all my creditors. What a huge relief! I went back to answering the phone. The real upshot of it was that I started carrying around a little book, and every time I spent money, I'd write it down. At the end of the day, I'd add it all up. Then I started taking those numbers and building a spreadsheet. Over time, that spreadsheet provided me with history, and I could see figures represented as percentages of the total. I could determine if I was spending too much money eating out, on clothes, or on groceries—or even if I should be spending more in any of those categories. After a few months, it gave me a picture of who I was as a person at that time.

I don't carry around a little notebook anymore (although I think my wife would like me to), but I pull all the numbers from my online bank statements. I still go through the monthly numbers, and I have a cash flow chart that covers over twenty years of history. I also have a schedule for net asset value, credit cards, and debt with rates and payment dates.

Without these tools, I wouldn't have a clue about where I was or what I could or couldn't do. My guess is if you're not doing that at home, you're probably not very good at it in your business. Just guessing, but you probably rely on cash flow to

---

iii   Mundis, Jerrold. *How to Get Out of Debt, Stay Out of Debt, and Live Prosperously.* Bantam: New York, 1988.

pay your bills. As a leader, you need to know where you are, and only numbers will tell you.

ACTIONS TO TAKE

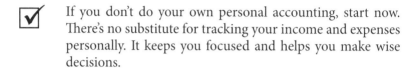 If you don't do your own personal accounting, start now. There's no substitute for tracking your income and expenses personally. It keeps you focused and helps you make wise decisions.

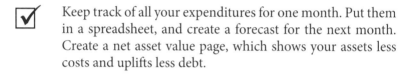 Keep track of all your expenditures for one month. Put them in a spreadsheet, and create a forecast for the next month. Create a net asset value page, which shows your assets less costs and uplifts less debt.

☑ Do this every month, and build an annual cash flow chart. This is a powerful tool for business planning, and it allows you to gain wisdom from seeing the effects of past choices. Relish the knowledge you acquire by studying the numbers, and make wiser choices because of that knowledge.

My Notes

_____

_____

_____

_____

_____

_____

_____

_____

_____

_____

_____

_____

_____

_____

BUILD A BRAND

NUMBERS ARE IMPORTANT, profits are important, and cash flow is important, but people will be drawn to you initially because of your brand. As a leader, you need to turn your vision into a business and your business into a brand. Think of impressive brands you know. Let's take Coke, Ford, Wal-Mart, Microsoft, and Apple. You picture the brand, the logo, before you see anything else. In today's digital age, attention spans last no longer than two minutes. You need to grab people's attention and get above the noise in your sector. You need to stand out—just like those household names. And you need to be able to do that in whatever country or sector you're in. That's what we did at Ober-Haus.

A brand can—and should—lead the business; it can even loom larger than the business itself. You need people to identify with the brand, to see it in their mind's eye, to recognize it in less than a second. If you can do that, you've added tremendous value to your business and set yourself up to grow rapidly. And when it's time to exit the market, it's that brand, as much as anything else, that buyers will be purchasing.

How do you rise above the noise? A name, a look, a color. What can stand out to represent you in the crowded marketplace? You need to grab attention, and it needs to reflect who and what you are. If you are lucky, you might stumble upon it one night while watching TV, or you might have to get a brand consultancy firm to help squeeze it out of you. Either way, you will need something unique and attention grabbing to make yourself visible. Once you have figured out your brand, build on it. Hire an agency that can get the word out. You don't need to know how to do that. Remember, you're the guy with the vision. You need to make sure others communicate your vision in the best way possible.

HERE'S THE DEAL

In 1993, I was renovating one-off single apartments and homes and renting and selling them. I had a few people working for me, and we were making a decent amount of money. Not a lot, but decent. The market was getting crowded, and we really weren't doing anything that anyone else wasn't doing.

One night as I was watching TV and making notes in my journal, I unconsciously started writing my name and my wife's last name: Oberschneider and Hauser. I found myself combining the two names and drawing an ancient crest in the middle. The result was Ober-Haus, and it was an epiphany moment that changed my business for the next fifteen years. "Ober" means "head" or "top" in German, and "Haus," of course, is "house." Literally in German, the name means "House of Lords."

The beauty of that name is that all these small Central and Eastern European countries spoke different languages and had different cultures, but at their core, they were all historically Germanic. My competitors all had local, bizarre-sounding names that, while good in one country, could not transfer to other countries. Ober-Haus would translate well in every country. It was perfect for a cross-border real estate company. That was our advantage.

We took that name and created a brand with guidelines to follow across the countries we expanded into. It worked. It allowed us to grow where others could not get traction, and that brand became recognizable everywhere we went. Our brand actually became bigger than our business.

Today, I'm looking at my phone, and I see hundreds of messages on social media from people telling me how they are going to make me rich, help me create a personal brand, and teach me how to increase my sales and become a millionaire. Now, I know there are a lot of smart people out there, but I wonder how many of these millionaire gurus have actually made the millions they claim. Few, I suspect.

Or maybe I'm a dinosaur and just don't get it. Maybe I've missed the whole media entrepreneur thing because I'm not tech savvy enough—but I'm learning fast. Meeting my new Nigerian friend John-Paul through the internet, reading blogs, and exchanging ideas across the world changed the way I view doing business. Yet whether you are doing it digitally or making calls and putting up posters, building any brand takes time, and you need to be consistent with your messaging.

But don't be fooled. You can waste a lot of hours getting hooked by the messages these ads preach, and in the end, you'll probably be no closer to building your business than when you started. In fact, they might convince you that you aren't ready.

The formula, after all, is pretty simple: when starting a business, find some aspect of your business that uniquely identifies you, that distinguishes you from the rest of the market. Broadcast that element on a consistent basis until your brand is known. Generally, the key to building a strong brand is to provide some kind of pleasurable experience or solve a distressing problem for your customers. Your brand needs to convey that people will get either pleasure or a solution from you.

ACTIONS TO TAKE

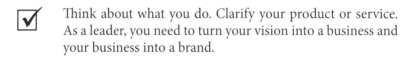 Think about what you do. Clarify your product or service. As a leader, you need to turn your vision into a business and your business into a brand.

☑ Remember, people have short attention spans. Grab their attention, and get above the noise in your sector. You need to stand out.

☑ Look at the competition, and consider how crowded the market is. Identify the aspect of your business that uniquely identifies you and distinguishes you from the rest of the market.

☑ Create a logo, a look, and feel that will make you stand out above the noise. You need people to identify with the brand, to see it in their mind's eye, to recognize it in less than a second. If you can do that, you've added tremendous value to your business and set yourself up to grow rapidly.

☑ Build that brand into everything you do. Broadcast it on a consistent basis until the market recognizes you.

My Notes

BASKETS OF BUSINESSES

IF YOUR CORE BUSINESS is a good one, it probably has more legs than you can imagine. You may quickly find opportunities to expand what you are already doing into another related business, which gives you diversity and a second source of income. Entrepreneurs are always looking ahead at the possibilities. They connect dots and lines where others don't see them.

Of course, your first business is your most important asset. This is the baby that will make or break you, so all your focus is on building a team and a brand and rolling out your product or service. And that's exactly what you should focus on. At some point, though, you will see that there are other aspects of your business that can be divided, or at least segregated, into separate businesses.

As I read John-Paul's book, *101 Ways to Make Money in Africa*, I got lost in the world of possibilities. The book is full of ideas, and John-Paul and his co-author, Harnet Bokrezion, are passionate about African entrepreneurship and driving growth on the continent.

Africa is a continent with a population of over one billion people. And it's not just its sheer size and population that make it exciting—it's full of natural resources, human capital, impressive talent, and consumers. To most investors and entrepreneurs outside the continent, Africa is still a virgin market and a dangerous place. There is uncertainty, massive corruption, terrorism, and, in some parts, life is cheap. It reminded me of what people used to say about Russia and the former Soviet Union countries: danger, car bombs, Russian mafia. If you can get your head around all that, below the surface is huge potential. What is really lacking in Africa is a knowledge base of business skills. But that is changing rapidly.

John-Paul and I agreed to Skype. I had read his book and was full of questions. While Tula's product wasn't working in London, I was keen on exploring his product as an African business, and John-Paul thought it was an amazing idea. But there were problems to sort out. What I discovered in our conversation was that while resources and a growing market of consumers made Africa a virgin market, the infrastructure for production was abysmal. As one of the major growers of fruit, Africa is also one of the largest importers of oranges and bananas. Not because it doesn't produce enough but because of a lack of road infrastructure, collection, storage, and processing. Fruit gets picked and then is left to rot. One idea led to another problem that led to another idea. There was plenty to do, and solving many of these problems would lead to other problems. This is an entrepreneur's dreamland.

HERE'S THE DEAL

When I was building, renovating, and renting apartments, I needed someone to manage them. Of course, I could—and did—manage them myself, but I realized that other developers and property owners might like to use a management service, too. Kind of a no-brainer. So a few loyal colleagues and I built a property management services business. It started slowly, then easily spread across all the countries we operated in—first for residential and then, as I built shopping centers, for commercial properties.

As my agency business grew and we sold homes to people, I found that we often had clients who didn't fit the lending criteria of the local banks. I realized I could sell so many more homes if my clients had financing. Naturally, we wanted to increase sales, so I started a mortgage company to help our clients buy homes. I became a loan origination business, selling off syndicated loans to the banks that wouldn't give these people credit in the first place.

By 2008, we had a retail and commercial real estate agency business, a residential and commercial property management services company, a mortgage bank, a development company, and a chain of hotels. Each of these was a separate business, each with different services and priorities, but they all flowed out of the parent business: Ober-Haus.

The beauty of this, of course, is that when it's time to exit a market, or when you tire of a company or feel it has achieved its potential, you will have the luxury of being able to pick and choose which ones to keep and which ones to sell. Separating your business into different baskets multiplies your options. Your eggs are not all in one basket, even though they came from the same chicken.

ACTIONS TO TAKE

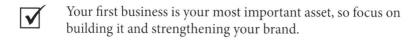 Your first business is your most important asset, so focus on building it and strengthening your brand.

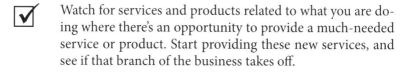 Watch for services and products related to what you are doing where there's an opportunity to provide a much-needed service or product. Start providing these new services, and see if that branch of the business takes off.

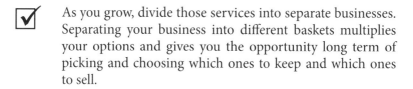 As you grow, divide those services into separate businesses. Separating your business into different baskets multiplies your options and gives you the opportunity long term of picking and choosing which ones to keep and which ones to sell.

My Notes

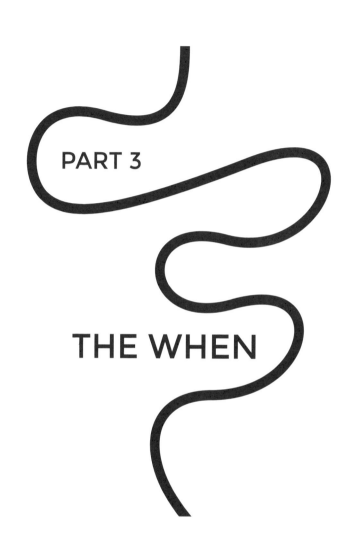

PART 3

THE WHEN

WHEN IT'S TIME TO FOLD

DON'T KNOW ABOUT YOU, but frankly, I'd rather be persistent than dogged. Being persistent means if the idea isn't working, you don't give up, but you do change the way you are doing things before you try again. Get out and start over. Doggedness—like insanity—means doing the same thing over and over and expecting the results to be different. Many people get the two concepts confused.

Tula met with the insolvency guy I introduced him to, and he had to face his family and friends and tell them his decision. It was a hard thing to do, and he knew that, for a while, they would probably be upset and refuse to speak with him. But they would forgive him eventually, and it was better to get it over with. He had turned to me for a loan, and I refused. Lending him more money wasn't the answer. His original business idea might have been a good one, but he had executed it poorly, and now he was under a huge weight of debt. There really was no way out of this except to close down the business.

Yet Tula struggled with the temptation to doggedly try over and over again, expecting a different result. He was still married to his idea. Even as he met with insolvency lawyers to wind up his company, I noticed he was still pushing out Facebook ads asking people to try his products. I could only imagine what was going through his mind. He was desperately trying to hang on.

When I was a trader on Wall Street, I learned a valuable lesson. Cut your losses short, and let your winners run. "The trend is your friend," my boss Herby used to tell us each and every day. Most investors do the exact opposite. It's the same in business. At least when you are trading, the pain of being wrong is quicker. Businesses take longer to bleed, and you might die a slow death like a frog in a boiling pot. Tula was that frog. And as the water boiled, he was still blogging and posting Facebook ads.

HERE'S THE DEAL

When you think about it, the math is simple. If you had a hundred dollars to invest and you minimized each loss to only ten percent, you could trade a hundred times before losing it all. A hundred times at something is a long stretch. Chances are if you were disciplined enough to do that, eventually you would be right, and the winners would make you enough money to cover your losses. And if you pyramid on your winners and add to them as they grow, you could even multiply your gains. Most people do the exact opposite.

People become attached to their businesses. They had a reason for starting their business in the first place, and they struggle to admit that they were wrong. So they hold on and continue to throw good money after a bad idea. They always think their losers will turn around, and they usually don't.

The English hotel I'd invested in was trading badly, but because I had been successful so many times before, I thought I could adjust things and succeed this time, too. For years the company hemorrhaged money, and I thought I could turn it around. I threw more money at the problem. But the circumstances were different this time, and I couldn't accept that I was wrong. Basically, I ended up working for the bank for free trying to save this asset. It was a waste of time and energy. Losing takes its toll, both emotionally and financially. It's better to stop early, regroup, and start again rather than trying to prove something. Being stubborn doesn't make you smart. Pigs are stubborn, and they get slaughtered. I've been a pig a few times in my life, so I know what that feels like. Don't be a pig. Ask yourself these questions:

1. Are you losing money?
2. Are you emotionally tied to your decision?
3. What would be the consequence of getting out?
4. What would be the consequence of staying in?
5. Are you being honest with yourself?

If your business isn't making money—if you must constantly subsidize it with more funding—don't fool yourself, your investors, or your bankers into thinking it will come around. Be brave and honest. There's no harm in being wrong and failing. If it's not working, chances are it won't. In life, in business, in equity and futures trading, just get the hell out before the failure becomes spectacular.

ACTIONS TO TAKE

☑ Know how much you are willing to lose, and stick to that commitment.

☑ When you reach your limit, get out. Losing takes its toll, both emotionally and financially. It's better to stop early, re-group, and start again rather than endure a lingering death. Don't make excuses. People become attached to their businesses, so they hold on and continue to throw good money after a bad idea.

☑ Be honest with yourself, your investors, and your bankers. It's better for everyone to know what's really going on. This builds trust, and it's the right thing to do. It's not a failure to be wrong and shut down your business. The only failure is not getting out when you should.

☑ Don't be afraid to regroup and start again. One false start is not the end of your entrepreneurial ambitions.

My Notes

_____

_____

_____

_____

_____

_____

_____

_____

_____

_____

_____

_____

_____

_____

_____

_____

Notes Contd.

_____

_____

_____

_____

_____

_____

_____

_____

_____

_____

_____

_____

_____

_____

_____

SELLING TACOS IN AFRICA

WHEN I FIRST SET OUT to write this book, my title was just a metaphor. I wanted to write a book that could help and inspire people. Then I met with Tula and John-Paul and started a dialogue about Africa.

One day, I sat looking at a big map of Africa on the desk in my office in Oxford. I flipped open the map and pointed at a spot. My finger landed on a lake in Ghana, specifically on Lake Bosumtwi. Near the lake stands a tropical city of 1.7 million people called Kumasi. It's famous for its flowers and plants and has a high school, university, and teaching hospital. For people who know the city, it is in decay. At least that's what Wikipedia said about it last I looked.

But if you happen to be an expat looking for a night out, you will find pizza, Indian food, and even an El Gaucho restaurant. Being a lover of Tex-Mex food, I was curious if you could get tacos or a burrito there. Nope. No Mexican burritos. So if you're aching for Mexican food in this 100-degree tropical city, you're going to be disappointed. You might have to go somewhere else.

If I had tried to make a living writing business plans in New York City in 1992, I would never have made any money. New York is a competitive financial market with a lot of smart consultants and corporate finance guys. In Estonia in 1992, I was one of the only guys in the field, and I could charge what I wanted. It was what I like to call a blue-sky market.

My trip to Estonia was an adventure in an emerging market surrounded by other emerging markets that had fallen out of the former Soviet Union. I would eventually do business in all of them. As I continue to read more about Africa and meet with people, I see huge similarities between the former Soviet Union countries and the continent of Africa. There are major differences, of course, but the sheer size, by comparison, is overwhelmingly attractive.

And like all opportunities in emerging markets, as I have seen, the window will close quickly. But for a while, many entrepreneurs will have blue sky and be the only game in town. That makes all the difference before the wall of liquidity and banking comes rolling in.

Basically, you'll make three critical decisions in your business:

1. What you do.
2. Whom you do it with.
3. And most importantly: *where you do it.*

There may be a stench in the streets in Kumasi, but people are eating. Even in poor countries and cities, a distraction from everyday life is often a meal out. So why not Mexican food? There's no one else in the market, and it's a big market. In fact, there are opportunities like this across the entire African continent.

Back in 1992, I was no business genius. I wasn't even thinking about being in business on that square in Tallinn when I met Sergei. I was just out enjoying myself and admiring the architecture and the blonde Estonian women. But Sergei needed a business plan, and I helped him. No one else could do that at that particular moment in time. It was *where I was* that made the difference. I solved Sergei's problem, and that was the start of my business.

HERE'S THE DEAL

When you are thinking about a business or sector to launch in, look for a market or opportunity where competition is lacking. Opening a quick service food business in one of London's hottest sectors means trying to muscle your way into a crowded market. There are thousands of guys doing the same thing. You are not going to solve anyone's problem by launching another fast food chain.

I look for blue sky. I look for that African market where little competition exists. Blue sky means a market or opportunity where you are free to create and explore before everyone else catches up. It's where there is little competition and pricing is still inelastic—in economics, this means demand doesn't fall regardless of a rise in price. Writing my business plans in New York would have given me nothing, really. Writing plans in Eastern Europe after the fall of the Berlin Wall was easy money.

In 1992, I charged what I wanted. My new friend Sergei asked me to write a plan for his new shop to present to a local bank, and I was off to the races. There were no expert local financial consulting firms back then in these markets, and banks wanted business plans for their fledgling loan committees. I went from asking Sergei for $500 to asking an Austrian industrialist $50,000 for his plan two months later, and by the first summer, I'd made a pile of money. We developed shopping centers at development yields of 18 percent, and years later sold them at cap rates of 5 percent. This meant a huge uplift in shares, and fortunes were made.

As an entrepreneur, I take time to consider the potential size of the market, what the competition is doing, and how far they have gone. I consider what I bring to the table that is different—a new technology, service, or marketing strategy. If you are to succeed, there must be something unique about what you are doing. Be prepared to keep changing it to stay ahead. Markets change quickly. Be ready and flexible. But always start with an edge.

The business plans I wrote back in 1992 opened up other opportunities, increased my network of contacts, and introduced me to the main lending players at the banks. Those connections would later propel my businesses forward. Every dot connected, whether I knew it or not. But I was there. I showed up.

Hot markets are tempting. They look promising and always seem easy to enter. I look at the crowdfunding market today, and yes, it's tempting. I'm equally mesmerized by all these people on social media telling me they're going to make me a millionaire if I just click on their free video link. That's pretty cool. Yes, it's hot out there, and internet entrepreneurship appears to be growing. Fast food is crazy. But no one is making any money because they are all competing for the same sites, and restaurant property rent is way above where it should be as a percentage of sales.

And yet! And yet, there are a lot of people going into those sectors, and there are more to come. Be wary. A hot market is both crowded and competitive. Remember, by the time the market is sizzling hot, the tide has already risen and taken people to the top. The trick is to create and explore before everyone else knows the territory.

Decide where you are and what's missing near you. What are people lacking? What can be improved? What's coming? If you are alone, you will either be rewarded almost immediately, or you will find out how stupid your idea is pretty quickly. Neither are bad results.

You will have far more success opening a cool fast food taco stand in Ghana than in London or New York. You will be alone, and that's a great advantage.

ACTIONS TO TAKE

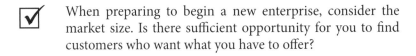 When preparing to begin a new enterprise, consider the market size. Is there sufficient opportunity for you to find customers who want what you have to offer?

Evaluate the competitive landscape. Are there thousands of others already doing what you want to do? If so, this crowded market is not the place to rise to the top—the first-comers are already there.

Ask yourself if the barriers to entry are easy to overcome. Can you start small? What does it take to give your idea a try?

Are you introducing something new to the market? If you are to succeed, there must be something unique about what you are doing. Be prepared to keep changing it to stay ahead. If your analysis shows you do indeed have a blue-sky market, jump in with both feet. Remember, quick success *and* quick failure are both good options. And always be ready to start again.

My Notes

_____

_____

_____

_____

_____

_____

_____

_____

_____

_____

_____

_____

_____

_____

_____

_____

THE TEST

I**T'S TIME TO WRAP UP** Tula's story, and I wish I could promise you a happier ending. But a happy ending is still possible—the story of Tula as an entrepreneur isn't over. As Tula and I continued to talk, it became clear he had no idea what he was going to do. Like a lot of entrepreneurs, he wanted to do everything at once and wouldn't give up. He was mesmerized by all his "friends" on Facebook and "likes" on his web page. But these were not showing up on the spreadsheet.

There are only three ways to fund a losing business: more debt, more equity, or not paying suppliers or employees. I can't think of any other ways. No one was going to lend Tula any more money, and he was not able to sell any more equity, so he was doing the only thing he could do. He wasn't paying anyone, and that only leads to tears and anger.

I explained that he had to list all his creditors, figure out the percentage of his debt that he owed to each of them, work out how much he could realistically pay them each month, and call them. A daunting exercise but one that would work. I'd done it myself years ago. Facing your demons builds character.

"What about Nigeria?" I asked him.

"Yes, people would love it in Nigeria," he said, "but I'm here now." He felt trapped and wouldn't look beyond his situation.

His business was like if I'd tried to sell business plans or consulting services in New York. It's not going to happen. You need to sell tacos in Africa.

We talked more, and I remained firm that I wasn't going to lend him any money to get him out of trouble. "Meet with your uncle, and put him on a payment plan. Then go to Nigeria, write up a business plan, and start small," I told him. "Take with you all you've learned from your mistakes."

Sadly, I was more excited by the possibilities than he was.

With my experience, I knew what those markets could be like, and with the right timing, the tide would lift entrepreneurs like Tula high above the watermark. But he wanted those magic beans. He wanted someone to bail him out of his problems. I couldn't do that for him.

There are no magic beans, I'm sorry to say. I know that's not what anyone wants to hear; it's not what Tula wanted to hear either, but it's true. Tula will only be successful when he faces his demons, takes a different path, and starts again. It's not a quick fix. Real success takes time. He will need to understand there are no shortcuts.

But remember, Tula's fear doesn't have to be your fear. Your story can have a happy ending. If you take the tools I've given you in this book, you can be the one to jump into the blue-sky market—to (metaphorically speaking) sell tacos in Africa.

What do you really want in life? It's a question that most people think about every day, whether they realize it or not. Personally, I think everyone wants the same thing: to be happy, to control their lives, to live free from financial worries, and to have a career they love and are excited about. Those are all good things to want.

But if you do what everyone else does and follow where everyone else goes, you will be like everyone else. You probably won't have those things that everyone wants. "Being like everyone else" is a crowded space. Competing in a hot market is tough.

In 1987, I had no foreseeable successful future and no real plan for my life. I felt trapped in a job, a routine, doing the same thing and waiting for something different to happen. That's insanity. We've all been there. But nothing different was going to happen if I just waited. I bought all the books with the five-point plans. But eventually, I found a much better way. I took a leap of faith, and this path brought me to even better places than I could have imagined.

An entrepreneur is a modern-day explorer—a person with a vision or goal in mind, going somewhere they have never been before. That's what I've always considered myself to be. But to make that vision happen, I needed three things: first, *to take a leap of faith*; second, *to have a vision and get good at telling stories*; and third, *to be willing to start small and do anything, anywhere*. Entrepreneurs make "their" thing "your" thing. And when you do that, people follow you, and you become a leader.

When I think about how I started with $400 and created successful companies from scratch attaining a total value of roughly 200 million euros, I'm astonished. I remember how fun it was and how time just seemed to fly by. Those eighteen years came and went quickly. I had gone on an adventure, like an explorer, and built these businesses in uncertain market environments, in countries with different languages and cultures that I didn't understand. Like me, Eastern Europe was finding itself.

Every situation is different, and business sectors are different, but I believe there are fundamental similarities in every journey. As I've written this book, I've had to look closely at myself in the mirror. What if I had to start all over again? I've done some amazing things, but that was yesterday. My office is full of pictures and press clippings, books, trophies, artwork, and fancy gizmos from my business days to remind me of who I am. But what about that line in the first chapter of this book? My claim that you could "drop me anywhere with $400, and I could start again." Like the line in the John Wayne movie *True Grit*, "That's a pretty bold statement for a one-eyed fat man," and that idea is keeping me up at night these days.

I've been feeling restless. I feel like Columbus waiting for my ship. So I'm planning an adventure, utilizing the same principles that I'm encouraging you to implement in your own blue-sky market. This new venture is still in the early stages, but I'm hoping that, very soon, I'll be starting over in Africa with $400 in my pocket to replicate my success. At each step along the way, I'll be using the paths I've given you in these pages. I'm at a place where I need to take the first step in another direction. I have to jump off the high dive one more time. I hope you will, too.

Final Notes

_____

_____

_____

_____

_____

_____

_____

_____

_____

_____

_____

_____

_____

_____

_____

_____

ACKNOWLEDGMENTS

THE ONLY PERSON BRAVE ENOUGH to hold a mirror in front of me at critical moments is my wife, Marlene. And as difficult as it is sometimes to see the truth, it's good to have a brave and honest person by your side holding up the mirror. So I thank my wife for her strength. I am also grateful for our son because he changed my world and made me a better person. I also thank all the people at Ober-Haus Real Estate, Hauser-Oberschneider, Schlossle Hotels, and Capfield for helping me build successful companies and accomplish the unthinkable. Finally, I thank God every day for guidance and strength and for the second chance he gave me.

ABOUT THE AUTHOR

PAUL OBERSCHNEIDER is a seasoned startup entrepreneur and property financier who has personally built businesses worth over $200 million. Since 1992, he has helped start a bank credit department, founded a mortgage company, and built the largest single-branded real estate company across five countries in Central Europe. He also developed a portfolio of shopping centers and hypermarkets in Eastern Europe, constructing over two million square feet of retail space. Paul retired, aged 49, before the financial crisis of 2008. Over the last two years, he's grown a chain of nineteen fast food restaurants in London and is involved in the Oxford entrepreneur community, where he serves as a mentor for startup entrepreneurs and as a speaker.

Paul's philosophy of business is simple: to be a successful entrepreneur, touch as many lives as possible by creating companies in uncontested markets where employees, customers, and communities are all winners.

Join Paul for more valuable insights, articles and video courses at:

www.pauloberschneider.com